Affiliate Marketing & SEO for beginners box set

Simple, smart and proven strategies to make A LOT of money online

Table of Contents

Affiliate Marketing for Beginners

Simple, smart and proven strategies to make A LOT of money online, the easy way

Introduction

I want to thank you and congratulate you for downloading the book, "Affiliate marketing for beginners: simple, proven strategies to make A LOT of money online, the easy way".

This book contains proven steps and strategies on how to start an affiliate marketing business online that makes you money you money while you sleep. This book explains step by step, how affiliate marketing works, how to start and how to make a ton of money using affiliate marketing online.

If you have ever thought about making money online, or if you have a blog that you want to make some money from, I'm sure the first term you have come across is affiliate marketing. While the term sounds technical, its actually very simple. All affiliate marketing is, is when you suggest a product, service or information product, and people buy it, you get a commission, it's as simple as that. But the power of affiliate marketing can be one of the best ways you can make A TON of money online, because the commissions can be as high as 75% of the price of the product. This book is a guide to getting started and making A LOT of money online, it tells you everything you need to know, including how to find affiliate products, how to get traffic and how to make the sale that ends up making you passive income while you sleep.

Thanks again for downloading this book, I hope you enjoy it!

Chapter 1: Basics of Affiliate Marketing

If you have heard anything about running an affiliate marketing business online you are have probably heard such gems as "you can set it and forget it", "affiliate marketing is effortless", "just sign up and you can't go wrong." Then there is the final favorite, "making money with affiliate marketing is a piece of cake." take all of what you have heard and throw it out the window because it is not true. While affiliate marketing can be easy once you have learned the ropes and put in the work there is one thing you have to remember above all when starting out. That one thing is the same you will find with any business, you need to have the spirit of an entrepreneur in order to succeed. You will have to work at it and learn that the key to an affiliate marketing business is that you must have the patience to build your affiliate business and you need to do a lot of research to find the affiliate business that will best suit you. If you are not passionate about a product you won't be motivated to do your marketing strategies and if you are not motivated to do your marketing you will not make money. This book will help you have all the tools and keys that you need to make affiliate marketing work for you so that you earn a steady income from your networks.

In order to be successful in affiliate marketing you need

a basic set of blueprints to follow, which through the course of this book we will give you. You also need to have a strong urge and desire to learn new things every day. You will constantly need to think of ways to associate, with your affiliate marketing business. There are no bones about it gets started with an affiliate marketing business is like starting your own business. You will need to put in the hours and strive for success every day. Unlike the common image that is being projected by those who just want to take in your referral dollars, affiliate marketing business is not a walk in the park.

With all of that said, affiliate marketing can be very rewarding and once you put these basic strategies to use for you, it will make you money and that is the goal of any business. The very first thing you need to do in order to be a success is to make sure that the affiliate network you sign up for to market with is reputable. Like with anything on the internet affiliate marketing has the good and the bad and the last thing you want to do is to bog yourself down with working on a network that has a bad reputation or worse yet does not pay you on time for the work you have done.

While nothing is foolproof, there are some key things to look out for when looking at an affiliate marketing program to join.

True affiliate marketing programs do not have fees: Affiliate marketing programs are always free to join and the only way you will be paid is if you make a sale. Even if you join a program that is two tiered where you get paid a percentage of those underneath you. The only way you make money from an affiliate underneath you is if they make a sale and earn the commission from that sale.

There will never be a true affiliate marketing program that has a "membership fee", it is possible to come across programs claiming to be affiliate programs that charge a "set up fee" or try to sell you a "website to market with." turn around, do not pass go ignore these websites, becoming an affiliate should always be free.

Red flags:

- Promises of money with little to no work involved

- Pictures of lavish cars and other "proof" of lifestyles of the rich

- Pictures of earnings that offer no proof of where those earnings are coming from

- If it says it is foolproof, walk away.

There are typically four categories that affiliate marketing networks will fall into, A-list, Secondary, E-product and Indie networks.

A-list networks:

These are often considered the brand names of affiliate marketing. They are programs that have secure and well known relationships across the web and stay with the largest brands. These networks include:

- Commission Junction

- Linkshare

- Shareasale

- Google Affiliate Network (This is not Adsense)

- Pepperjam Network

As with anything you choose to do to in business, there are pro's and cons to be found within each choice you can make in network. The Pros of going with an A-list network, of course, are working with the big companies that they have and you will never have to worry about being paid. Big companies like this are good for the money. Most A-list networks will also offer you merchant datafeeds for use.

The cons of working with such a big network are that you will likely not have as custom an experience as you would with a smaller company. If you aren't a huge affiliate with them it can come across like they don't always care about your interests. They can sometimes be more selective, as well, so if you are new or have not yet set up a website that will cater to your affiliate marketing and what you plan to get clicks for, it can be tough to get approved.

Secondary networks:

These networks are smaller versions of A-list networks they get smaller brands and newer brands those which may choose to skip the A-listers and look for something with a little bit more personal management style.

The biggest pro with these networks is that they tend to pay more often than the A-list networks and you do get that more personalized style of management with them. Since they tend to get smaller affiliates to join them you are not constantly feeling like you are trying to fight with the huge shark to get your cut.

The biggest con is that you really have to do your research before joining secondary affiliate networks. Many of them will disappear almost as fast as they show up so make sure that you join one with a good reputation that has been around for a while. There is nothing worse than doing all the work and getting shafted when a network does not pay you.

E-Product networks:

These are networks that will only offer electronic products, ones that are downloaded and not actually shipped. These networks include:

- Clickbank

- e-Junkie

- Avangate

- White Paper Source

You will have to be careful and watch the products on these networks, some are good and some are bad it will just depend.

Indie networks:

An Indie network can be good because they are smaller and tend not to have a middle man management team that you have to go through. They tend to allow you to get a bigger cut of the pie since they do not have as many middle people to answer to in the grand scheme of things. The down side is like secondary networks getting paid can sometimes be a bit of an issue, so you really have to do your research on the exact network.

The biggest con to Indie networks is finding them. You will have to search and try a few different search parameters first. Ones that work so far:

- [keyword] affiliate program

- [keyword] "become an affiliate"

- [keyword] affiliate

- [keyword] associates program

- [keyword] "become an associate"

Once you have found an affiliate network that you're interested in, the net step to being successful in affiliate marketing will be creating and finding your niche.

Chapter 2: How to find a profitable niche

Finding a niche in affiliate marketing is perhaps one of the most important things you can do besides finding a network. You have to be able to know what the people you are trying to reach want and make yourself stand out among the crowd. So the very first part of finding your niche is, figuring out what products your site visitors want to purchase.

Don't overlook the obvious:

Many who are just getting into affiliate marketing have a habit of overlooking the obvious, if you are already passionate about something that can be your niche. If you already use products look and see if they are part of your affiliate network, nothing is easier than promoting a product you already openly and happily use. As an example, if you own a blog that focuses on food, recipes and doing different food or crafts you probably already use preferred pots, pans, blender, crock pot and so on. Start with looking for those products and promote those that you find. It will be easy to write detailed reviews and product information because you are familiar with the product and you already enjoy them Not only will the reviews be easier but they will be natural and genuine, this is something that visitors will notice and its proven that people connect better with this form of write up.

If your blog or website is already established you have a readership and its human nature to want to use the same things someone you admire does. If I am following your blog and using your recipes I will want to use the same tools of the trade that you do, so I want to be helped by knowing what you prefer. A method of keeping these items always in the forefront on your page is having a resource page that is easy to get to. It is a nice none pushy way to constantly remind your readership, this is what I use and here is how you can get them.

Use Amazon to your advantage:

Amazon is the largest online retailer in the world and lucky for the affiliate marketer amazon shares their best sellers. The Amazon best sellers list gives you the top 100 selling items in any category that you choose and you can narrow it down in their subcategories as well. If you are a pet blogger who wants to fit your niche into pets, look at the pet category and then you can find their top 100 selling cat items or dog items and so on down the line. If even that is not specific enough to help you find the right products you can narrow the search down further and see the top 100 dog beds and narrow it down as much as you need it to, sub category after sub category. To add another layer on to how useful this tool can be for you as an affiliate marketer, Amazon updates their sales information every hour.

Be a problem solver:

If you can help a visitor solve a problem you will have an easy way to make a sale. The question then becomes how can you find out what problems those in your niche have? Believe it or not, that is easier to do than it seems. A little bit of research will go a long ways and there are several sites to help those sites include:

Uber Suggest:

If you add, "How to" or "how do I" phrases such as that to your main topic you will find a listing of issues that people are looking to have solved. Select the problems that have solutions which can completed with a buy-able item and you have the perfect item to add to your affiliate marketing line up.

Always recommend solid products:

While we mentioned in the beginning of this chapter that you should start with recommending products that you use, there are some niches where there is going to be no way that you can personally use every product. The selection will just be too big to do that. For niche's like that you will just need to apply a little bit of solid market research to seeing how much other people love or don't love the product. Once again Amazon can come in handy through customer reviews and general feedback, as do other online retailers. Doing a little bit of homework can help in the long run to make you money through your affiliate marketing network.

Check out the competition:

A general rule of any business practice is to take a look at the competition, this is no different in affiliate marketing. Once again, do a little research and find out what other bloggers or website owners in your niche are offering for sale. There is a formula to follow to make sure your competitor isn't just throwing ideas out there, but marketing like you to drive traffic and results. This formula is:

- Pay attention to what is being sold above the fold (top of the screen without having to scroll)

- Check the review section

- Follow the paid keywords

- Research only those who have keyword overlap with your site

- Look for income reports (not all bloggers post these, but if your competitor does check it out)

Once you have chosen your niche is it important to stay proactive and stay on top of trends within it. The only way to be a success in affiliate marketing is to constantly be vigilant and stay with the current curve.

Chapter 3: How to build an affiliate blog in 9 easy steps

If you are reading this book so far and thinking, "I don't have a website" or "They cost too much to start up!" take a deep breath and relax there are a number of free or low cost platforms that you can use for your affiliate marketing. It is also not difficult to build websites anymore and many platforms do the hard work for you, all you have to do is input the information. Building your own blog or website is as easy as following the steps listed in this chapter.

Step 1:

Select a name. A good website or blog name is very important. In just a phrase you have to have something that hits on your brand, is descriptive and flows nicely so take some time to pick the right one.

Step 2:

Once you have decided on a name you will want to decide if you want your own website or blog, or if you prefer to use one of the many already in use platforms. There are free blog platforms such as Blogger or Wordpress as well as many others. A simple Google search for free blog or free website will bring up a large variety for you to select from if you chose to go with a free platform.

Step 3:

If you have chosen to go with a free blog site platform the next step is to create an account on the chosen site. A note about this method however is that while free is sometimes the only way to start out, if you plan on long term affiliate marketing you will want to give serious thought to getting your own domain for brand purposes.

Step 4:

While creating your own site is not free it will certainly give you more flexibility and administrative control over your website. It also helps with building a trustworthy brand name. Research in this area shows that many visitors are more likely to shop links from sites that are .com's or something similar versus a sub-domain. If you have chosen to go with your own site, you will need to register with a registration service such as Namecheap or GoDaddy, this usually costs around $10 per year.

Step 5:

After you have registered your site, you will need to find a hosting service. Most major registration sites will also offer hosting for a specific fee per month or discounted rates per year. There are some sites that offer free hosting, but there are often limits on how much bandwidth and storage you can use.

Step 6:

Once you have decided where you will be hosting your website you will need to set up the correct name server information. If you set up your site with the same service you registered on, chances are they will do this automatically, if not you need to input it manually. Name service information will look like this: It will look something like ns20.namecheap.com and ns21.namecheap.com.

Step 7:

Once the information has changed over you will be able to access your control panel to see what else you need to add to your website. If you have chosen to go with a blog format (which is the most common) you will then need to select blog software that you wish to use. Most hosting services will have a large range of formats you can chose from. A benefit of choosing from one of the more common formats such as WordPress is that there will be a large range of free themes to choose from.

Step 8:

Once you have installed the software onto your website that you plan to use and picked a theme whether it be a free theme or one you have paid for it is time to look at the plug ins that you can use to help your website. An example of plug ins that you will find useful for affiliate marketing are:

- Site Security

- Site Administration

- SEO (Search Engine Optimization)

- Site Statistics

- Formatting tools

Step 9:

After your site is set up you will want to create the first post for your content. After the first post you can make any adjustments that you might need to and add your affiliate marketing network information.

Chapter 4: How to become an authority

Now that you have picked your niche and have your website ready it can be easy to do what is called, "built the website and then forget about it" disease. Simply put, this is when a website or blog is built updated for a time and then forgotten about. Sadly, this is seen all over on the web you will visit a blog or a website, only to see that it has not been updated in years and this simply does not work with affiliate marketing. If you take part in this build it and forget it state of mind you will kill any money you can make through affiliate marketing, you need to forget this old web way of thinking and join in the new web way of thinking. The old way of thinking was that you could build a website, place basic information on it with links and not worry about it. The new web thought is much more interactive you can't just copy information not if you plan on making money through your website.

The key word here is content. Not just content, but fresh, consistent and updated content. Websites that get the most traffic and so the most sales through affiliate links are those that are always changing, always having fresh content and being improved. Visitors love to see new things, take part in new article discussions anything that they see as valuable when they come to your website. So give them that reason to come to you, give them that reason, to click on your affiliate marketing link. Every old school affiliate marketer knows three key reasons why they should keep their content updated and those three reasons are:

Reason number one: Search engines give websites that are updated often better rankings:

Search engines are an invaluable resource to any affiliate marketer because this is where people turn to find things on the web. When searching people want to find the things that are most relevant to them and in order for search engines that means making sure a website has, "good stuff" and is frequently updated. In order for search engines to see what "good stuff" is they have several different identifiers that they use, one is frequency.

When a search engine will check and see the dates that you post and if you have done frequent updates the search engine will mark the site higher up in results than one that does not update often because it will be seen as a consistent source of new information, the higher up you are the better chance at higher traffic drives from search engines you have.

If you think about this in terms of print, like a newspaper it can be easy to understand. When you get the Sunday paper you read it see it and enjoy the news it offers. However, if the paper were to be the same the next Sunday and then the next and the next and so on and so forth, would you keep your subscription? Would you keep reading the paper? Chances are you would cancel that subscription because you are getting nothing of value from it. If the content never changes and you have already read the content you will move on to something else, something that offers you new content. The internet is no different.

Reason 2: Give your readers a reason to come back, increases the percentage of sales

If a non personal thing such as a search engine thinks your website is outdated, why would a human think anything different? When a reader comes back and sees that nothing has happened on your blog for months at a time, many things come to mind, the business must not be growing, you must not care, you must not be innovating. You must not be getting any customers, so what are you doing wrong? Are your products bad? Are you a scam and not delivering the products? Is there something wrong with you? While none of this is likely true for you it is what readers will start thinking and if they start thinking like that they will not want to shop with your affiliate marketing network and then you will not make any money. Small changes like news updates, shop announcements, even just a little check in will show your readers that you are actively working on your business.

In short posting new and update translates into better chances of closing a sale through your network. While they might not be ready on the first visit however, when they come back and see new content, new deals something that shows them things have been in motion while they have been gone they are going to pull the trigger and you make the money.

Reason 3: You can track your website performance and see what has high interest and what has little interest.

When you have all the data in your hands, it is a lot easier to make choices for your affiliate marketing business. When you see what will work with customers and what will not you can change your format to more of what works to grow your business successfully.

When you do not update the content and nothing ever changes you will not be able to see if it is operating at peak performance or not. You will not know who is coming to visit your website or how many people come. When you add content you can use an easy to access tool such as Google analytics to look at your data, see which posts are being read and what posts about your affiliate marketing content are producing sales. It is important to be proactive about your website, it is the face of your venture so to speak.

Using these basic tips and building on top of everything else you are learning about affiliate marketing will ensure that you have an easy time making money. You may have to work to make sure that you make money, but it does not mean you can't have fun doing it and creating content about a niche you are excited about is always the fun part of the job.

Chapter 5: Getting traffic in 7 easy steps

Driving traffic is essential to the success of your affiliate marketing plan. If you do not have traffic you can't sell the products so sales and traffic go hand in hand. When you are new to affiliate marketing it can seem overwhelming to think about getting traffic, long established sites seem to have a lot of it and it can seem like you will never get there. The good news is that if you break down getting traffic into easy steps just like the other strategies we have covered you will find that it is easy.

Step 1: Choose a professional design.

While we covered briefly choosing the right template for your website, we will cover now while it is important to driving traffic to your site. When a new reader arrives to your blog or website you want them to see a professional image. This will go a long way to show your credibility, enforce your brand and increase the sales you can get. A professional design should be crisp, clean and should look good on desktops, laptops and mobile devices.

One mistake that new affiliates make when putting together their design is placing too many advertisements on the site. Readers will find too many advertisements intrusive. Always keep your advertising clutter free and professional. There are more ways to attract sales than just sidebar advertising, that can interfere with content. Your design should also encourage your readers to stay on the website for more than a brief look around, give a recent blog post feed and a featured post spot to show them what might be interesting to look at. The best place to put featured and related articles is at the bottom of blog posts.

Step 2: Make sure your website is SEO friendly.

While you want to make sure that your website is beautiful for humans to look at you need to make sure that the search engines mentioned in the previous chapter can find you easily. While updating content is part of the algorithm another important part is SEO. Many blog platforms such as WordPress already have built in features to make your site SEO friendly, like custom page slugs.

Ensure that your website theme has proper header tags that can be validated with HTML or CSS with no errors in them. Using plugin's such as All in one SEO or Yoast SEO will ensure that you are able to optimize every page and post to your website. These same plugins can also be used to create a sitemap which is easy for Google and other search engines to crawl and ensure you get a higher ranking.

Step 3: Write high quality articles.

It was Bill gates who once said that Content is King and that statement stands as true today as it did when he said it 18 years ago. While it's okay to make announcements and short articles once in a while the bulk of your website needs to be high quality relevant content. Remember to solve problems with your content like we mentioned in a previous chapter and in addition use he following as a guideline to high quality content.

- Always use images in your posts

- Create a strong title

- Keep an eye on grammar and avoid using too much "web speak"

- Publish honest reviews

- Consider interviews with people important to your niche

- Make quality lists posts such as "Top 10's"

- Consider infographics and other easy to share content to mix it up

Step 4: Interact with your readership.

Fans of blogs, websites or other social media like to feel like they are being heard. If they have an open relationship where they feel like they know you in some way they are more likely to buy products you recommend, it is about building trust. If you have questions on content that is on your site take the time to answer it. Thank readers who take the time to comment and in general be as social as you can. You can also interact with your readers by social media platforms like Twitter, Facebook, and Google+. If you want to be creative, consider doing reader interviews and making a content piece based on them!

Step 5: Make it easy for your readers to share your content.

Word of mouth is the easiest free way to spread content and get more visitors to your site. Social media is the biggest form of word of mouth advertising today and you should make it easy for your readers to share something that like on your page. The easiest way to do this for you and them is to integrate sharing buttons directly into your content. Once again, there are many plugins that can be used for this purpose and it makes it easy for you to install them. Just do a search of the plugins for your platform and find the one that works best for you.

Step 6: Grow your overall online presence.

One of the easiest ways to grow your online presence and drive traffic to your website for affiliate marketing is using an email marketing list. Encourage one time visitors to subscribe to your blog, post links to subscribe lists on all of your social media accounts and take the time to research email marketing software. This kind of software will not only drive new traffic, but keep loyal readers who will become the cornerstone of your affiliate marketing cash flow.

Step 7: Be patient.

When you are first starting out with a new website and new affiliate marketing the hardest thing in the world to do can be to wait. You want to see instant results and see the money start rolling in. Unfortunately, while you can make it easy for yourself to make money through affiliate marketing it is not a get rich quick scheme you have to have some patience. Keep up positive and fun energy following the steps in this book and you will see success. Have fun with the content, use raffle copter and give away some small items to bring more people in but always be patient.

The bottom line to any new affiliate marketer is to go in with a plan, keep the content quality flowing consistently and be patient. You can make money if you stick to your guns and put in the work. Once the hard work is done, it becomes easy to sit back and truly enjoy the work you are doing everyday. Being your own boss can be very rewarding with affiliate marketing.

Conclusion

Thank you again for downloading this book!

I hope this book was able to help you to build an online affiliate business that makes you financially free in every sense of the word. The internet offers countless opportunities to make money, and affiliate marketing is the fastest and easiest way to get started.

Finally, if you enjoyed this book, then I'd like to ask you for a favor, would you be kind enough to leave a review for this book on Amazon? It'd be greatly appreciated!

http://amzn.to/1snint0

Thank you and good luck!

Check Out My Other Books

Below you'll find some of my other popular books that are popular on Amazon and Kindle as well. Simply click on the links below to check them out.

SEO Basics: How to use Search Engine Optimization (SEO) to take your business to the next level of success

Social Media Marketing for Beginners: How to build a social media strategy that really works

Affiliate Marketing for Beginners: Simple, smart and proven strategies to make A LOT of money online, the easy way

If the links do not work, for whatever reason, you can simply search for these titles on the Amazon website to find them.

SEO Basics

How to use Search Engine Optimization to take your Business to the next level of Success

Introduction

I want to thank you and congratulate you for downloading the book, SEO Basics.

This book contains proven steps and strategies on how to use search engine Optimization to make your business a huge success.

This book introduces the readers to the world of SEO in the simplest of terms. SEO can be difficult to understand, but in this book everything from A-Z is covered. It explains what Search Engine Optimization is, why it is important, how search engines work, how to optimize a page or a website for a search engine, different types of SEO techniques, along with various tips and tricks to reap long-term benefits.

Thanks again for downloading this book, I hope you enjoy it!

Chapter 1 – What is Search Engine Optimization and how can you use it?

No matter what you do online, at one point or another, you will come across the word 'SEO.' Search Engine Optimization. So, what is this search engine Optimization? Why is there so much hype about it? Why does it matter, and what can it do for you? Why is it so important?

If you make a new website or a blog, a part of the process will be optimising it for search engines.

The standard definition for Search Engine Optimization is:

"Search Engine Optimization (SEO) is the process of affecting the visibility of a website in a search engine's 'natural' or 'organic' search results."

A few years ago, I made a website, and ignored the step where I could optimize it for search engines. I did not think I needed it. A year later, the average traffic per day on my website was somewhere between 5 and 9. My website was really well made. I made everything clear, from what it was all about to the services I offered. The website failed because I skipped one of the most important things. I didn't optimize it for search engines.

Search Engine Optimization is what you do to bring more traffic to your website. When you search for something on a search engine, like Google, the results you see are search engine optimized. Optimising your website for a search engine improves its visibility. It makes it easy for the search engines to find it, and for the people to find your website, page, or business. The most well-optimized websites are on the front page. Most people never look beyond the first three pages on a search engine. When you search for something, you get tens of pages with results. If your website is somewhere in the middle or the end, the odds of anyone finding your website are pretty slim. That is precisely why you need to optimize your website for search engines, and bring it to the front page.

The results you see on your search engines are primarily of two types:

- Paid
- Unpaid

The paid and sponsored results are highlighted and stand apart from others. For these, people have to pay to the search engine. There are charges associated with every click so it can be very, very expensive. Therefore, we focus on generating natural or organic traffic.

Search engines have algorithms and web crawlers that help them filter the websites so the results can be authentic and free of spam. The more authentic a website looks to the search engine, the higher it will rank.

In the next chapters, we will discuss the methods and strategies that will help you optimize your website or content for search engines to rank higher in the results, and to bring more traffic to your website. We will also discuss the different types of SEO, the difference between them, and how to ensure that your website gets indexed. I will also make sure to explain everything in the simplest words possible so you can fully grasp the concepts.

Chapter 2 – How Search Engines Work

A search engine is basically a program. When you search for something using this program, it uses the words you type and searches its database, matches your queries in its index, and brings you the most relevant results. There are algorithms involved in almost every step that ensure that the results you get are the most relevant.

In order to understand search engine Optimization, you need to understand how search engines work. We will start with crawling and indexing.

Web Crawling and Indexing

A web crawler is either a program or a script used by search engines. The crawler used by Google is called 'Googlebot,' and is the most popular web crawler today. The job of a crawler is to browse all the websites on the internet that are available publicly. It creates copies of the content it browses on the websites, to be processed by the search engine later onwards. They also help the search engines to keep their data up to date.

A search engine will eventually add your website to its database; you can also do it manually. When the search engine has discovered the URL to your website, or added it to its database, it will schedule it for crawling. There are several different factors involved here, and the list of websites is rearranged by an algorithm. Not all the websites that are in the database are crawled.

After the crawling comes the indexing. During indexing, which is also determined by an algorithm, words related to your document point to it. That is when you can say that your website has been indexed, or added to the search engine's index. Remember, search engines have algorithms that decide whether or not to crawl or index pages.

Difference between Search Engines & Web Directories

Although the terms are often used interchangeably, search engines and web directories are not the same.

A search engine creates the list or index of websites automatically. Web crawlers keep the content on the search engines up to date.

A web directory is usually an organised list of websites. Unlike search engines, it is maintained and updated by human beings, not web crawlers. While they may not be as comprehensive as search engines, the websites they list are usually free of spam. It is hard to trick them because the lists are maintained and updated by humans, not automated scripts.

Stop Words

When the entries are being indexed, the search engines delete the stop words. Stop words include words like: he, she, it, a, and, the, is, are, etc. that are of no use in terms of search. As a result, the search becomes much more efficient, quick, and fast. In the past, this was important because memory was expensive. Now, even though the memory is cheap, time and speed matter a lot more than they used to. So, to expedite the search process, the stop words are deleted.

Term Stemming

During this step, the suffixes are removed. This is also to speed up the searching process. For example, the system will look at the page and find similar words, like: forge, forged, forging, forgery, etc. What it will do is index the term 'forg' instead of indexing all the similar terms.

Index Entry Extraction

After term stemming, the index entries are extracted and a shortened version of the page is stored. It looks less like the original page and probably does not make any sense if it is read, but it is never presented for reading. The resulting page only makes the searching of entries easier by removing the irrelevant entries.

The Working of a Search Engine

There are many different search engines available today, and all of them work in different ways. There are some basic steps that are followed by all search engines, although they constantly update their search methods. For instance, Amazon has its own search engine, and while it is mostly the same as other search engines, it has one key difference: it uses categories. But this is just to give you an idea of how search engines differ from each other. Our main focus is on search engines like Google, Yahoo, Bing, etc. where you can get your website listed, indexed, and ranked higher.

Then comes the searching and matching. When you search for a term, the search engine will look for it in its indexes, match the term, and bring forth the results.

Page Authority

The pages are also ranked depending on their authority. Authority pages get the top rankings, so you have to ensure that you make authority pages. The authority of a page depends on two things:

Content

Links

Content

This is the stuff that you write on the page. It includes key words and is crawled by the web crawler.

Links

Links tell the search engine that your page is important. If different websites or pages link to your page, the search engine will realise the importance of your page. The more links you have, the more authority your page will get. You can think of these links as votes; votes that will help you rank higher in the results. The more votes you get, the higher you will rank.

Now, to make your business successful, you have two goals:

1. Keep writing content with the right key words to promote your page and make it easier for it to be found.

2. Try and build links to rank higher in the search results and build more authority for your page.

Doing the things mentioned above is called Search Engine Optimization. In the next chapter, we will discuss the different types of SEO.

Chapter 3 – Different Types of Search Engine Optimization

As with all other things, there are two ways in which a page can be optimized for a search engine. They are:

Black Hat SEO

White Hat SEO

Black Hat SEO

Black Hat search engine Optimization is the unethical way. It is not recommended, but it is important to understand it so that you know what to avoid when optimising your page for a search engine. Black Hat SEO is basically the abuse of tactics, techniques, and strategies of White Hat SEO. The techniques are used aggressively to rank higher in the search engines. Search engines have their own rules and guidelines, which are not followed or obeyed in Black Hat SEO. The pages are filled with key words, also called 'keyword stuffing,' doorway pages are added, content that is actually irrelevant and misleading is used, etc. But the results of Black Hat SEO are only short term, and the websites that do this end up getting banned by the search engines and are removed from their lists. Black Hat SEO does not bring any long-term benefits.

How to Avoid Black Hat SEO

Here's how to avoid Black Hat SEO:

Key Word Stuffing

Filling your pages only with keywords with the goal to rank higher in the search engine's results may help you rank higher quickly, but will eventually get you banned by the search engine. So, avoid stuffing your page with key words.

Doorway Pages

This is another way to abuse SEO. A fake page is created that tricks the web crawlers and results in the website ranking higher, although this page is invisible to the users. For long-term success, your goal should be to create a quality and valuable website that improves the experience for the users. Do not create any doorway pages.

Invisible Text

Long lists of keywords are added on the pages to trick the crawlers. The colour of the text is kept the same as the background of the page so the text remains invisible unless highlighted by the user. This is another unethical technique that should never be used.

White Hat SEO

White Hat SEO is the ethical SEO. When you use the techniques, tactics, and strategies of SEO as you are supposed to, and, as regulated by the search engines, then that is called White Hat Search Engine Optimization. It involves the use of key words, building links, backlinking, keyword analysis, etc. It results in long-term benefits because the authority of your pages continues to be strengthened, and there is no risk of your page getting banned by the search engines.

In the next chapter we will discuss how to optimize your page for a search engine using the White Hat Search Engine Optimization techniques.

Chapter 4 – How to Optimize your Website/Page for Search Engines

Let's jump right into Search Engine Optimization!

Keywords

Keywords are the words that people type on search engines to search for something. During Search and Match, the keywords of the user are matched with the content on your website, so it is very important to make sure that you have the right keywords on your page. But how do you choose the right SEO keywords?

Do not be too generic

The keywords that you use on your page should not be too generic. If they are too generic, your page will get lost in the results. People looking for it will not find it easily, and the ranking will go down. If your business is about a shampoo, then the keyword 'business,' or 'hair,' will be too generic. The word business will result in different businesses, and the term hair will lead to hundreds of pages about hair. If your website is about an herbal shampoo that is for volumizing hair for women, then your keywords would 'volumizing,' 'hair,' 'shampoo,' and 'herbal.' These keywords increase the scope.

Do not be too specific

Do not be too specific with your keywords either. Your goal is to increase the overall scope while staying on the topic. If your keywords are 'how to,' or similar, then websites like Wikihow and HowThingsWork will take the lead, and your website will be lost in the results. The keywords need to be balanced so while the scope is broad, the results still lead to your website.

Be Consistent

The process of ranking higher in search results takes time. The keywords you use should be consistent with what your website is about. You have to stay focused and approach the same thing in different ways. The keywords should not be about something that you focus on once in a while only. If your keywords are focussed on what you do regularly, are consistent, then voila! Your website will rank higher! Whatever your website focuses on, whatever your keywords are, write about them as often as you can.

Titles, Subtitles, and Descriptions

Do not keep the keywords limited to the general writing. The titles should always include a keyword or two. Keep the titles short but make sure that there is a sprinkling of keywords in them. Ideally, a title should be between 10-14 words, and should start with a keyword.

Subtitles can also be utilised for keywords. You can use more keywords in the subtitles.

The description is where the rest of the content is. An ideal density of keywords is said to be 1%, which means that there should ideally be at least one keyword in every 100 words of description or content. For better search engine Optimization, make sure that the keywords are used in the first 3 lines, or the introductory lines, of the page.

Keyword Research

Before you start using keywords, you should do some keyword research. It gives you an idea about the relevant terms that people search for, so you know what people search for when looking for something, and then use those keywords to help them find your page or website. For example, when you are typing something in a search engine like Google, you will notice that the search engine also suggests something before you have even finished typing. At least half of the time, what you are searching for shows up. Google calls it Google Suggest. You can also use Google Insight or Adwords Keyword Estimator to get an idea about the keywords that people search for. In Black Hat SEO, people just research and find out the keywords that people search for and stuff their pages with them, but the same technique of researching can be used in an ethical way and for your own benefit. You can include this in your research to learn more about how people look for things, what terms they type, when looking for a business like yours, and then include them in your keywords. Because the end goal here is that the user should be able to find your website or page.

URLS

The URL of your website or the specific page should also include the keywords.

Build Links

Finally, try to build links. Get similar and relevant websites to link back to your website or pages. If the content on your website is good enough, people will automatically link back to it. If you write a good article on giving a back massage, someone writing about getting rid of back pain and suggesting massage may link back to your page. Similarly, if you offer a good hair product, a website that contains information about hair may link back to your page to let people know that the product you offer is good. Alternatively, you can bring attention to your page. You can ask people to link back to your page, not only for building links but also to help others. A good linking techniques used by websites is offering discounts. For instance, website B shows a link to website A along with a 5% discount offer, which makes the people on the website B go to website A. Social media also helps by playing a vital role in this. People share and re-share good content and offers, and this also helps build links.

Chapter 5 – Keeping Up with SEO

Search Engine Optimization is not a one-time thing but an ongoing process. To continue to rank higher, you need to continue to produce good content to stay in the limelight of the search engines.

Have a Blog

Blogs are places for writing, no matter what you write about. You can write daily, weekly, or monthly on a blog. Search engines keep their data updated, and also note how frequently a page or website is updated. So, try to get new content on your website, page, or blog at least 5 times a week. All this content should also be search engine optimized.

Plan Ahead of Time

Don't just take it as it comes. Have everything planned ahead of time. This gives you time to build upon and improve your content. It ensures that you are consistent.

Stay Up to Date

Keep yourself updated with what's going on in the world. If your website is based on mental illnesses, then keep up with the world of mental illnesses. Find out what research is being done on it, shed your light on new research, and throw in your two cents. As soon as the word spreads about something new, people seeking answers search for it. Your goal is to make sure that the right people find your website too, and that they get to see what you have to say about it and what you have shared.

Give Them Something More

If your website is an online business, not every post should be about selling stuff. If you are always trying to sell something, if you are always focusing your articles on what you sell, people might be put off and get the feeling that they are being forced or cornered. So, if your website sells a volumising hair shampoo, it is better to just write about hair problems like hair dryness to bring them to your website. If they do visit your website, they will browse around.

Give Them Something of Value

If you write with the goal of getting people on your website without providing value, there will be no benefits. Search engines also notice how much time a user spends on a page or website. If the users leave quickly, your page gets down voted. So you have to provide content that is valuable. It should be good enough that people give it their time, actually stop and read or browse around. The more time they spend on your website, the better.

Linking Back

It is quite the opposite of backlinking, but the results are similar. Link back to good websites and pages. Search engines already know about the good and authentic pages, and when they see that your website is sending people to those pages, they up vote your website because they realise that your website is giving the users more quality. The focus here is on 'quality,' so make sure that you don't just link back, but link back to quality websites, or it can be counter-productive.

Add Photos

Most people have short attention spans, so having photos on the websites can help retain their attention for a while longer. In addition, photos relevant to the content increase the overall visual appeal of the page. People, today, have short attention spans, more so on the internet. This gives you a very little time to capture their attention, so you have to do all you can to make them stay. When adding a photo, rename it and use a keyword in the name.

Keep It Interesting

Do not bore the visitors. Whatever content you put on your website, keep it relevant and interesting by using interesting headlines, catchy titles, and brief descriptions.

Word Count

Most search engines ignore the pages that have less than 500 words. Whatever you write about should contain at least 500 words so that the search engines and crawlers take it into account.

Meta Data

The Meta data contains information about what your page includes. Most website hosts have made it easier for the clients today and removed the manual work, so all you need to do is ensure that the meta data also contains the keywords that are appropriate and relevant to the information offered on the page.

Use Categories

This is mostly for blogs. The blogs can touch on a variety of subjects, so instead of having a huge unsorted archive, use categories and sort out all the data. It makes it easier for the users and visitors, and also gets you noticed by the search engines.

Chapter 6 – Search Engine Optimization and Ranking Tips

Here are some important tips that will help you improve the Optimization of your page and rank higher.

Readability

The content you write on your website should be readable. It should engage the visitors. It should sound like a human wrote it, not a robot. Robotic tones make people lose interest and result in them bouncing off your page, which harms the rankings. Readability takes several things into account, including grammar, formatting, and tone.

Grammar:

When the content is grammatically incorrect, it offends the readers. When it is grammatically correct, it is more readable.

Formatting:

The content should be properly formatted. Do not use colours that blend into the background, or are so bright or light that it is difficult to read them. For instance, it is very difficult to read text that has the colour 'lime' on a white background. Use headings, subheadings, paragraphs, and bullets to make things easier on the eyes.

Tone:

The tone should be maintained properly, be it professional or conversational. The conversational tone is more engaging, but the tone you need to use depends on where it is being used.

Again, in short, write like human beings write.

Do not change the domain name of your website

One of the factors in the ranking of your website is its domain name. The older the domain name, the more authentic it is. So do not change your domain name every often or throw away a good one. In addition, changing your domain name too often also results in loss of visitors.

Get your website indexed

If your website is not indexed, you can do it manually; and it is completely free. Following are the links to the popular search engines where you can submit your website:

Google: http://www.google.com/submityourcontent/

Yahoo: http://search.yahoo.com/info/submit.html

Bing: http://www.bing.com/toolbox/submit-site-url

Keep your website active

Search engines use crawlers to keep their content up to date. If you do not update often, or at all, the crawler will have nothing to report for it. The search engines want to keep their databases up to date, and that is an opportunity for you to improve your rankings as well, because by updating frequently, the message you send to the search engines is that your website is active, alive, and kicking.

Load Times

Only keep the relevant data on your website. Too many photos, animated images, gadgets, effects, etc. slow down the loading time of the page, so to make sure that your page loads faster, remove anything and everything that is not essential to it. Sort everything out and put things in relevant places, so that the website loads faster. The less content it has to load, the faster it will be. Websites with too much non-essential content do not load properly or completely on slower connections.

Focus

Stay focused! The website should focus on one main thing and stay focussed on it. It can branch from there on, have secondary topics, but it should never lose focus of the primary thing it is about.

Chapter 7 – SEO in a Nutshell

Here's a quick run through search engine Optimization from the beginning to end.

- You begin by finding out who your audience is. Once you have identified your audience, you have to find out that what do they search for when they need products or services that you offer.

- There are databases on the internet that have this information. They help you find out what people looking for your products or services search for. This is a part of the keyword research, and does not infringe on anyone's privacy, because the only information they provide is what your audience searches for, nothing personal about them.

- Then come the common phrases that people search for. They are common, hence, when used, they will bring organic traffic to your website.

- But, it is important to also find out other similar websites who use the same keywords. Know your enemies, or competition. You have to know who you are up against to beat them.

- Keywords! Keywords are the words that people use in the searches, words that you can get from online databases, Google Insight, etc. to bring your audience to your website.

- Links are votes of authenticity. Authenticity brings you to the top of the rankings. So, you have to get other websites to link back to you to increase the authenticity of your pages, and you have to link back to quality pages to let the search engine know that your website focuses on and provides quality.

- Content: It includes everything that is on your website. It should be well-written, formatted, and must contain keywords. No matter how good all the content is, if it does not have the keywords, people will not find it. If people do not find it, you do not get any visitors and the ranking goes down.

- Engage and Capture the Interest: Whatever content you put on your website, it should be interesting and engage your visitors.

- Blogs: blogs are perfect for search engine Optimization. A website can be limiting in terms of content, but that's where the blogs come in. A website can only contain so much content, but a blog is all about content. You can update a blog frequently, and if it is a part of your website, your website will benefit from it too.

- Consistency and Focus: Lastly, consistency and focus are important. You should keep everything consistent, stay focused, and not lose track of what your website primarily is about.

- Be Patient! Search engines take their time. If you want to reap long-term benefits, you will have to be persistent and patient.

Conclusion

Thank you again for downloading this book!

I hope this book was able to help you understand and learn search engine Optimization.

The next step is to start optimising your pages for search engines and start generating organic traffic.

Finally, if you enjoyed this book, then I'd like to ask you for a favor, would you be kind enough to leave a review for this book on Amazon? It'd be greatly appreciated!

Click here to leave a review for this book on Amazon!
http://amzn.to/1tapefo

Thank you and good luck!

Check Out My Other Books

Below you'll find some of my other popular books that are popular on Amazon and Kindle as well. Simply click on the links below to check them out.

SEO Basics: How to use Search Engine Optimization (SEO) to take your business to the next level of success

Social Media Marketing for Beginners: How to build a social media strategy that really works

Affiliate Marketing for Beginners: Simple, smart and proven strategies to make A LOT of money online, the easy way

If the links do not work, for whatever reason, you can simply search for these titles on the Amazon website to find them.

SOCIAL MEDIA
MARKETING
FOR BEGINNERS
How to build a social media strategy
that really works
BRIAN CONNERS

SEO
Basics
How to use Search Engine
Optimization to take your business
to the next level of success

BRIAN CONNERS

AFFILIATE
MARKETING
FOR BEGINNERS
Simple, smart and proven strategies to make A
LOT of money online, the easy way

BRIAN CONNERS